The Aloe of Evening

John Knoepfle

Indian Paintbrush Poets
Colorado

Copyright © 2015 John Knoepfle. All rights reserved.

Acknowledgment

Grateful acknowledgment is made to the *Illinois Times* for the first printing of "meeting mr lincoln."

Cover design by paperwork

Indian Paintbrush Poets is an imprint of
Pearn and Associates, Inc., Book Publishing
1315 Kirkwood Drive, Apt. 905
Fort Collins, Colorado 80525
For manuscript submission, query by mail
or e-mail victorpearn@ymail.com

Library of Congress Control Number: 2015945515

Knoepfle, John
The Aloe of Evening, by John Knoepfle
ISBN 978-0-9897242-5-8 paperback

Printed in the United States of America
1st edition

for Peggy Sower Knoepfle

contents

communal poem	1
letter to an old friend	2
for thea in july	3
high waters	4
neighborly	5
alfred e smith banquet televised	6
tuesday at the café moxo	8
where are they now	9
just saying whatever this morning	10
last lines for carol	12
what to say this thanksgiving	13
2010 on christmas	15
christmas at hickory glen	16
about fathers	17
2012	18
on this day	20
where are you	21
old memories	22
night of the meteor shower	23
so one more day	25
where is the title	26
well I had something in mind	27
what to say about this	28
this silent moment	30
soothing lines for this morning	31
odd saturday in may	33

say this tell what happened	34
hospital moment	35
an exquisite moment	36
it is a strange emptiness	38
good news this day	39
meeting mr lincoln	40
friday the thirteenth	42
what john told peggy	44
great serpent mound revisited	45
so still this winter morning	46
lines taken from an old notebook	47
reading the heavens	48
september 7th	49
good friday	50
what were you saying	52
the day after tomorrow	53
blessing to fill a long life	54
now we are toward winter	55
the parade has ended	56
so much and so little	57
somewhere beyond desire	58
a farewell to august	59
lines for a hand crafted book	60
scratch out anything	61
what happened to this computer	63
it used to be fanciful	64
speaking of being tired	65
sometimes with little to say	66
mail poem	67
sometimes you just keep writing	68
words at the edge of time	69

communal poem

here is a retreat
a sylvan place
flowers and green shadows

the day is cool
there are dogtooth violets
a social of bluebells

the world recreating itself
a damp fertile place

it is time to abandon
the caution of success
time to turn the radio down
denature the tv screen

time to listen and watch
listen and watch

letter to an old friend

hamlet you should have lived
beyond the painful time of your youth
your old friends
perhaps you would still have them
yes horatio and those old true
classmates from wittenberg
the ones who would never betray you
your mornings spent reading their e-mails

not coping with isolation
not the business of a king
not a hamlet idling on the computer keys
adrift in places better unknown

but I am saying more than I want to
more than I should now
among the slain in elsinore

where to go on with this
story of a drowned girl
the skull of a jester found in a grave
students caught up in affairs of state
beyond their comprehension
jerked aloft in hangmans knots

what will we see tonight
what tomorrow will see us
opening our eyes again

yesterday the play ended
there could be no curtain calls

for thea in july

now the dark afternoon hours wane
the gray sky thickens in the west
and the illinois summer is hot
and we are returned from sacramento
went there welcoming the latest
family gathering for the little one
child of dino and erika
born in a city in india

sleeps when she wants to
wakes when she wants to
cries when she is hungry
never long and her milk
the pumped and the breasted
all the richness the generations
on this solitary planet can offer

this rare child of mumbai
with her wide blue eyes
and I say her hair the color of queens
and when she smiles
the adults around her melt
I say my dear rare child
thea I say here is your world

high waters

what to say this morning
unspeakable news this morning
more rain in the forecast
and the mississippi
broad and as high as I have ever seen it
and the wild missouri
straining the levees in the west

radio cackling
interviewer wants to know why
gay writer doesn't write about gays
well he doesn't feel like it
that should have ended the interview
but she had this time slot
kept the questions going
already answered for everyone

talk about the atom bomb
reactor building up in syria
bombed to smithereens

thats the morning news
as for me let me tell you
my heart is the same as yesterday
and has been these
odd ninety-two years

saw two lovely girls
granddaughter and friend
off for texas saturday
dropped them and daughter
at st louis airport
has lindys plane inside
imagine flew the atlantic in that

neighborly

there was a softened breeze
easing over our houses
this warm thursday morning

everything was so quiet
all my neighbors sleeping
it seemed so and even
the dogs must have been dreaming
not furious in the yards
when some poor cat eased by

and I should yawn
as I half slumber here
be kind and forgive me my friends

oh may your pleasant hours
refresh your own lives waking
and a gentle evening
comfort you when you sleep

alfred e smith banquet televised

the annual dinner
and john mccain at the right hand
of edward michael cardinal egan
and on his left barrack obama
and the program director was eghan mcguinnes

what a surprise when mccain was introduced
he made a stand up presentation
had the guests at dinner
holding their sides laughing

I couldn't believe it
the man hardly a day before
locked in a punishing debate with obama
but there he was and I shook my head

how could anyone match him
but then obama came on
and did the same

they both had remarks for hillary clinton
had her convulsed with laughter
daubing the tears from her eyes

and then the cardinal closed out the evening
there in his scarlet canonicals
the third stand up comic of the night

and then a parish priest said the after grace
a grandson of smith
and this was the solemn moment
and the end of the evening

but there was more here for me
because my mother had known alfred e smith
both from saint james parish the school there
administered by the christian brothers

yes and across the street
the church with its awesome interior
where the professional paul bearers
lofted maggy finns coffin on their shoulders
and slow marched it into the rain outside

my mothers cousin
the only irish blood relative I ever met
all my nine uncles and aunts
gone before my time

tuesday at the café moxo

1
it is tuesday again and i am with
the spanish speakers at the café moxo
this in springfield on an overcast morning

2
at a loss for ideas
i stare at a blank page
what a checkered life i have had
it is always like this with elders
wandering somehow in a time warp
as if we were living on some other planet

3
the virgin of guadalupe
she was dressed in the robes
designed for an aztec princess
gave juan an armful of roses
though it was not a season for roses

4
but i will not go on
this story so well known
with those lovely chants and songs
and the roses so unexpected

5
but today is beverly's birthday
and we sing happy birthday in spanish

where are they now

I remember that comfortable
rise and fall of the pacific
the steady plunge and recovery
the old salts adjustment
beyond sea sickness

you wish somehow
you had forgotten
how to walk the deck
the easy compensating knee bend

where are my shipmates
john from cincinnati as I was
we shared a dinner
at the coronado
with my next door neighbor
marianne who was now a wac

kelly who sang when irish eyes
are smiling as we drifted
with a dead engine
under suribachi yama

swede who saw the shell
whistle over
my landing craft

just saying whatever this morning

how to start with nothing
what world is this my darling
presidential debate last night
baseball pennant races

cardinal laid to rest in chicago
that was so long ago
it could only be yesterday
beloved compassionate man
often amused with himself

where are we going this morning
irish bands on my player
sets your toe keeping time

well I have been busy
though I can't say at what
well making the big old bed
marriage bed this morning
why did shakespeare
will his wife the second best bed
never been able to understand this
no one else either I guess

this is my world this morning
well no not quite here are those
obituaries and someone
veteran of the pacific theatre
someone local was he someone
I saw over the reefs at okinawa

why do old memories persist
as if life stopped at that moment
yes the air raid on manus
I was in the hospital then
but nothing was hit
well maybe a palm tree

I must hurry on it is almost
two hours until the noon tide
when the sun will be overhead
and there will be no shadows

last lines for carol

at four oclock the birds in the garden
attend to their psalms
it is that sort of day
beginning with a consecrated hour

overcast perhaps

a weekend saturday
we will go to the farmers market
this morning later

what to find there
all that our far flung neighbors
have drawn from this rich black earth
our central illinois legacy

what am I saying
all that is alive this day
should lift us up

should hurl us all heaven high
beyond our needs beyond
all that we could ask for

hold me kindly in your thoughts dear
as I write these lines for you

what to say this thanksgiving

well of course a family gathering
we do not discuss politics
what to say then this thursday
well we all watch detroit lose
that is a tradition
and usually have a beer watching
or maybe two and chips or pretzels

I the grandson of immigrants
swiss and irish grandparents
but my children and grandparents
they through their mother
they are pilgrim americans
one of their ancesters
his name was john howland
he fell off the mayflower

and these generations before
these heads bowed in grace
their kentucky ancesters
fought on both sides
when civil war bled this nation
knew bull run and after
apache raiders and after still
drill master at west point

what to say off the starboard side
slid the bodies in their canvas sacks
for their creators keeping
fathomed in the deep pacific

and this last week uncle jim
spoke of foxholes in viet nam
and this morning peg editing
a persian novel a remembrance
figures dancing
so many lights from a bridge

what to say offering thanksgiving
shell bursts on the horizon
pray for enemies
for a grace filled day
the healing of ancient wounds
the easing of troubled minds
the protection of innocence

it is two thousand twelve
time for a day of shared kindness

2010 on christmas

the train is up and running
the tree works there is a blue lit candle
set in every window
the snow came yesterday afternoon
brought four soft inches
all the presents have been handed out
sons grandchildren gone home contented
some getting older
choose carefully for grandma grandpa
a good day for a good day
and last night an outstanding choir
leading with a welsh carol
now overcome with cinnamon rolls
we put in a sated time towards supper
christmas day 2010
my record of the moment
a little groggy from lack of sleep
two oclock last night shutting eyes
and tomorrow the anniversary
fiftyfour years now
who would have thought
well all things are possible
sometimes all things are just possible

christmas at hickory glen

all these folks in their eighties
many ninety and more
troopers in the game of life
cautious not to fall
and end up in the hospital

at dinner a cheerfulness
good fellowship
graced with gallows humor
how tough we all are

well we are not made forever
meantime the lord of all creation
swaddled in a manger
offers us transcendent joy
and we respond with carols

about fathers

well striking lines
not knowing where
they will take me
where this afternoon
what avenues of the mind
I have read about
a young man
who did appreciate
the greatness of his father
until he tried to become him
well I can tell you
all fathers here
wept when they heard of it

2012

thursday morning—after the election
what to say
still recovering
so late watching the returns
sweep for democrats
as it turned out

I have been going through
a stack of old verses
wondering when I wrote these lines
hoping I did not publish that one
oh well we strive for perfection
it is the nature of our imperfection

suddenly lonesome
perhaps how a president feels
after the acceptance speech
going back to the hotel
crowd left cheering
wondering where home is

goodbye good luck
I say this to myself
I say this to all who voted
winners and losers
goodbye good luck

goodbye mr president
god keep you safe
god grant you wisdom
the very special insights
that only a chief executive
needs for correct decisions

the dawn woke with birds singing
and the seconds kept
a ponderous time
ticktock ticktock ticktock
tick tock

on this day

bright sun soft wind
young woman saying goodbye
young husband sober as his call to arms

I try to write these lines
come to a close
sadness drifting in like hunger

we are just running on
just so my morning

where will they be
where at this sundown ending
where will they know joy light
hope faith pardon love peace

when there is nowhere to go
it is possible
the healing will begin

you have to believe this
more than anything else

where are you

so hard to answer this
our limited time here
imaginings so far beyond
what it is we can know

what will become of us
who will find us
perhaps a thousand
say who were these people
the ones frozen in these fields
what did they dream of
want from this life

yesterday evening wow
a storm to end all storms
great sheets of rain
crashing thunders
lightning to wake up the blind

now it is peaceful
overcast sky
what is taking place
all that rain
arctic melt down perhaps

where did you all go
it is lonesome here
I do not know why all this
just down in the mouth today

old memories

where have you gone old friends
ray who became a doctor
tom who flew b-29s out of england
and the cartoonist for the sun times
who married toms sister
and charlotte my first date
we saw trail of the lonesome pine
some who broke my heart
and some I may have hurt as well

where to go from here
so much forgotten down the years
lost along the way
with grandparents and parents
three brothers all the aunts and uncles
now in another time
where in time we may all meet again
flawless hopefully beyond all time
oh yes companions beyond time
should I look forward
or stand and wait
knowing they will be there
beyond whatever time I know

night of the meteor shower

two-thirty saturday morning
this old man stood on the backporch
wrapped in his bathrobe
went out there in the cold
for a night watch
beneath the dark heavens

time for the meteor shower
detritus from haileys comet
streaking the placid sky
rare predictable event

but not this night
a gauzy curtain of thin white cloud
draped from horizon to horizon
ended all hope and perhaps
my last chance oh well
what does that mean old goat

well just spinning lines
this is what I can do
always with that pressing
desire they would be
better than they are

still far to the east
there were sudden short streaks of light
so fast you had to wonder
did you see a meteor or not

were you asleep or not
where were you if you were not
searching the sky in the early dark
lost for a moment in outer space
becoming someone other than
the man you know you are

so one more day

maybe the last I will spend here
sitting at this computer
old surly buddy
oh well change comes

your hair turns white
you fall off a porch
well goodbye old house
goodbye prairie patch
blooming under my window
thistle bonanza for gold finch

not the final goodbye
just to say not in jerome now
living at hickory glen

at ninety-two
yes you could say waiting

where is the title

how is this
a writer not wanting to write
what is it
somehow just being tired
saying well maybe tomorrow
but tomorrow when it comes
will be the same as today

why this fatigue
desire to sleep of a morning
please explain this to me
I would say it is the pills
but I have not taken them yet

get up get up
the morning is wasting
redeem the time
make this an hour to remember
this day this side of eternity
aha old man rouse up
into the fray once again
oh quihote with your broken lance
oh roland with your great horn
oh anybody sleepy

it is already time for a nap
oh the confusion
I already took that
well how about ending this
abracadabra cadabra abra
what is the next possible word
shhhhhhhhhhhhhhhhhhh

well I had something in mind

but whatever it was it is gone now
well what do you expect
this brain is ninety plus years

even to get something down
the very attempt is a triumph
and who knows another day
everything will come back to me
a chinese junk with bamboo sails
carrying my cargo of old thoughts
memories of my perilous teens
all the lovely girls I knew then
and those steadfast teammates
double dating on the soft weekends

yes I have lingered here
but I will stop now praise the lord
some days are like this one
full of regret and thanks

what to say about this

now my eyes are tearing
the left eye especially
overflows warming my cheek

shivers too down my spine
perhaps a draft
wafting from the steamer

and I don't know either
what music from the radio
inhabits the kitchen

now a voice on the telephone
this with a flash of lightning
boom of rolling thunder

talking about me
what to do about my itches
that time of year
house too dry for an old man

want to scratch my behind
can't do that in a civilized country
only scratch there
if no one watches
an honored custom
where poets give readings

but how about this
male cardinal oh colorful bird
working along the fence
sings me away from a cheap
preoccupation with myself
saying all sorts of things here
concealing others in the quiet
painful tolling of my heart

this silent moment

the furnace is humming in the basement
there is a ringing in my ears
and the clicking of computer keys
and the creaking of the chair back

outside baffled in yesterdays snowfall
an illusion of soundlessness there
cars drift by on the street
as if the drivers were lost in dreams

this empty page
I so wanted to say something

what has changed since yesterday
the handsome butterfly cup
a crack in it this morning
it will not be thrown out

some things should be held as priceless
like recalling a stranger
who went out of his way to help you
someone you are unable to name

soothing lines for this morning

so I will not describe
this coffee shop
I have done so
how many times
the years passed

but what to say then
well I have an ache in my back
left shoulder blade

Im beginning to feel like job
old body does not know
what to do with itself
how to get better on its own

now a muscle in my arm
cries to heaven
as I guide this pen for another line

oh how pain takes you
back into your secret self
not something you want to share

but lets think about that
what of an offering
you can parcel it may be
for those who suffer more than you

friend I in a miracle of creation
transport my aches
my bad right hand
my muscle pull in the back

wherever these may inhabit me
may they be transfigured
as a soothing aloe for your pangs
whether you are my deserving friend
or swaggering enemy

be cured be healthy
smile in a new dawn light
come alive and be more human
walk in the grace of heaven forever

odd saturday in may

how to do that
whatever that is
I don't know
what I do know is
this is saturday
the last in may I believe

well now the phone rings
I try to answer my cell
return the call on that
am told the mail box
what the hell is a mail box
Im on the phone
not trying to call the postman

I see now the word box
has a wavy green line under it
not this box
but the one below the box
where it says "I am told"
I am told but there are
strange thoughts in my mind
having to do with boxing day

well today I learned
the spanish for cupcake
well now I can say that
madalena yes cupcake
I sang to my wife
ola madalena
she says cool it
big boy

say this tell what happened

when was that
when was what happened
I don't know but it took me
four lines to get here

are you angry with yourself
yes I guess so I have to admit
and can you say why
no not exactly not really

have a slight headache
it seems I always have a slight headache
has to do with being eighty-eight
yes that must be it
how do you like this instead of a reason

who are you talking to

beats me some imaginary *reader*
—who changed the typeface?—
there is some evil impulse
something in the machine itself
something hooked up to the wall
wanting to leap out and destroy thought

reader the old faithful typewriter
the one still there in the basement
that one would never shift typeface
would never betray a friend

we must have come too far too fast
that must be it

hospital moment

the doctor said
how are you

she said I feel like
I'm having labor pains
but I'm too old for that

husband said
don't bank on it

nurses said
teeheeheeheehee

an exquisite moment

what does that mean
exquisite importance

wait I will look up exquisite
well here is a surprise
how about beautifully made
of such delicacy as to arouse delight
acutely perceptive
intense as in a pain
and it had an old meaning lost now
carefully sought or selected

hmm need to look up exquaerere
hmm to seek out
[I have to seek out to look up hmm
not hmm dummy to seek out]
well yes go to the indo european roots
the old tried and true
american heritage dictionary
has those roots
which root oh yes quaerere
I need to seek quaerere

root not listed
not in the ninth webster collegiate
don't look there

well guess what
the old faithful heritage
trumpets it means "to seek"

but having sought quaerere
quaerere turns out to be
a latin noun of unknown origin

doesn't that just freeze your ass

it is a strange emptiness

as if time went somewhere else
the sun did not seem to set
but then no one had seen the sun rise
and there was no moon
the brilliant sky not this night
because there were no stars
no bright patterns for the reading
dipper or dragon nothing we could read
a time of emptiness before the famine
friends let us take care of one another
listen to familiar voices in the night

good news this day

I put the dream catcher
up into the light
and look at this now
I already caught one

meeting mr lincoln

here in springfield
that is to say the one in illinois
not a massachusetts town
on the eastern seaboard
yes the one in illinois
where vachel lindsay imagined
the president walked at midnight

well he does as I can witness
only a week or so as I remember
yes early in april—I met him
on sixth street just to the south
where the old capitol is
yes it was in the morning though

will mrs lincoln be having
her strawberry levee soon
I said just to say something

he said why yes but you know
you have to wait on the season
yes you have to know
where the strawberries are growing
and when it is time for picking them

yes he said thoughtfully
you have to know when they are ready
and when they are not

I wished him the best of times
his one moment and forever
he touched the brim of his hat then
and said goodbye with a smile
I thought he must be going
for a roll call or a vote
sequestered in the capitol senate
or perhaps to tell stories
all afternoon in his law office

but when I turned to wave
goodbye to this great man
I knew would be president one day
he had vanished
and no one was walking the street
no one on that strange morning

friday the thirteenth

this is the time of year
unlucky for some I imagine
a coincidence of misfortune and date
some uneasiness down the ages
I have heard from
that sick thirteenth apostle

well what to say
don't suppose anyone into hell
executives whose stare
glittered with coins
stride so high they would not see us
shuffled under their feet

cut to the chase will you
examples could go on for pages
what did you dream of last night

I dreamed those images
dancing in my restless hours
sleeved their batons

how to describe slow hours
beyond the need for mantras

it is not easy to be lucky

can you imagine
not imagining can you define
emptiness beyond definition

where I am going
yes I have been there for a while
last night the alarm did not ring
the neighbors dog did not bark
there was no sound of wind or rain

where are you everywhere
when you are nowhere

what john told peggy

I was living in a place like this

I had been injured
I met this white rabbit
it was downstairs in the lobby

the rabbit knew about it

he spoke to me and was concerned

he told me about problems rabbits have
then on the fourth floor where I live
I met a dog

like the rabbit he spoke with kindness
when I woke I was happy

great serpent mound revisited

this year returned to ohio
where peg and I courted once
a half a century ago
it was a dreamy afternoon
resting our heads
on the flank of the good serpent

interesting that idea
how a serpent could be friendly
but yes in egypt and babylon
and among mayan and aztec
it was always thought so

and here in ohio the good serpent
keeps a lunar time
calling to each of us
along the road north
that swings through space
and joins the milky way

we can walk the serpent's home there
the dust of the evening stars
trailing beneath our feet

so still this winter morning

what is happening
blue sky white roofs of houses
white lawns clean snow
etched scene beyond painting
old man walking bundled against the cold

primordial stillness
as if sound were taken somewhere else
as if suddenly all life had ceased
the world rolling without purpose
through meaningless space
timeless inarticulate nameless

someone come to me
hold me in her arms
tell me my life is still there
if not in mine in her heart at least

where have I come from this morning
I remember it was six-thirty
yes I recall that and it was cold
and now I do not know how to stop these lines
abandon this page
knowing what I could not know
a wound so deep there could be no pain

there is a resolution
I leave it to this silence
the phone ringing suddenly

lines taken from an old notebook

didn't know where
it was going to end up
the blood of the world

I imagine I am somebody else
and that somebody is somebody else

history keeps coming in again
ringing a little bell
history is the salvation army
dressed as santa claus

beautiful books
when will they cease to exist
the height and width
of all that we can say

the time span of literature
spring again and again
gives it depth
knowing and not knowing

the covenant
of a marriage bed
verbs of responsibility

oh the abrasive beauty
the moons reverence
shining in the ruins of your eyes

reading the heavens

when I have seen
the first star rising
I will tell you
what life holds for us

when I have seen
the last star rising
I will tell you
what eternity can be

september 7th

the cool breeze
comes into this study
wants to lie down
go to sleep on the carpet

well perhaps thus is so
perhaps not and you say
well I can hear the wind
the big cottonwood
shakes its leaves
papery now with early fall
falling before the time

the air is sucked ice on my arm
I know this dark night
how shallow this life is
I am thankful so gentle
a thing as an autumn breeze
summons me for this moment

I should not complain

good friday

so quiet here under rain
all night rain trailing into this day
gray sky and stillness
no traffic on fillmore this morning
many sleeping late I imagine
others shaping for easter
brushing their teeth for candy
raspberry eggs coated with chocolate
or flocks of m and ms
for grubby hands later on sunday

there will be the sunday dinner
the special effort given
roast beef or traditional ham
for the rising this morning

now I wait the public stations
too wet outside this noon
will be indoors at little flower
and she the one this young saint
would not broad brush suffering
she knew it so personally
how it hurt too much to gloss
with any easy pieties

so the nails in the hands
the broken ribcage
thorns jammed into the forehead
the savaged feet

theresa noumann bled on good friday
I once saw the stained bandages
this saintly unprepossessing woman
she would gather the cigarette butts
the g.i.'s dropped in her yard
they could be recycled
small pleasures for her brothers

I doubt I would have done that
but then she was the one with the wounds

what were you saying

you are saying why all this bother
well I don't care and also
you can learn a lot reading tobit
but that is for you to discover yourself

be cheerful everything turns out well
old tobit gets his sight back again
and his young son finds a lovely wife
and all debts are paid on the ready
and no one practices extortion
or usury or anything like that

and our political electeds
ought to be ashamed if they know this book
and cheat and posture anyway
as we know so well so many of them do

yes each new day comes and sickens
and the terrible monster that frightened tobit
slobbers on its hostile beach
and the great angel left shaking the dirt off his feet
and old tobit dies blind
and the lovely girl never marries again
and even the little dog is sullen

you are saying what dog
well go ahead read the book yourself
it is all about justice yes to the core
and honesty and faithfulness and
yes something that happens in babylon

and may yet again praise god

the day after tomorrow

what happened
the years piled up
values changed
old friends drifted away

days grew longer
where to turn
how tedious the nights became

everything was wrong
something like that

a man alone with his prayers
trying to be still
so difficult to do that

blessings to fill a long life

who would have thought
so many years
so many adventures
generosities from strangers
hand given to the helpless sometimes

need to rejoice
need to be grateful
need to turn from the past
face into the future
short as this will be perhaps
this doorway to eternity

yes some days are like this
brimming with hope
generosity beyond merit
time left for giving thanks

now we are toward winter

advent on the horizon
but for the tremble of the last leaves
a stillness of stopped time
a breath waiting to be taken
as if the heart were resting
and all life were put on hold

I don't know perhaps
I am living this moment
beyond the end of time
is it possible time ends

the radio is busy in the kitchen
knowing all about the news
I remember directing tv news
wrote once that at that moment
the world was rested and at peace
it only seemed so of course

how many wars since then
how many widows widowers
lost children wandering ruins
grandparents without hope
husbands searching in rubble
wives clasping thin air

there is a light in the east
it is that time I guess
the time for waiting
hoping for something to happen

the parade has ended

how do you walk out of yourself
beyond the trail of words
enter a space without image
or perhaps abandon time
that ticking face of imagined hours

be able to consider
the far curve of some horizon
a sundown without shadows

where I will come perhaps
upon an indescribable moment

when my eyes will see nothing
and my heart amazed
does not hear its own beating

so much and so little

it is two-thirty now
our rainy afternoon
so quiet it is almost the first creation
but of course the telephone is busy
the tv is rolling some old movie
there is a hum in the computer
the chair creaks and there is
another universe
somewhere beyond this gray day

I don't have to tell you
you and perhaps deny it
friends where did our creation lead us
where did we ever come from

now a telephone conversation ends
bye bye always the last word
now someone screams on the television
gives up his tongue to drugs
a veteran of bad decisions
where will he sleep tonight

and miguel d'escoto how about this
raises a pencil in his right hand
and calls the u.n. general assembly to order
a maryknoll father
he was foreign minister of nicaragua
appointed by the sandinistas

and the rain comes down
and the rain comes down

somewhere beyond desire

where do you go
when there is nowhere to go
when you are the only one
who can spell your name

your old friends from college
those sweet dates
who were smarter than you were
but so polite you never knew

what is that bell ringing now
that summons to endless time

one day you wake up I guess
and hear cheering
yes a big crowd
those you hurt perhaps
who shake your hand now

and you know you are home

a farewell to august

where to go from here
something remembered from last night

thinking about that moment
marys reply to the archangel
angel saying as we have it in latin
ave maria gratia plena
those reassuring choriambs

our english equivalent from a drill sergeant
hail mary full of grace
our high school cheer leaders
waving their pompoms

and her answer behold the handmaid
quiet as the hours before morning

and what did that mean handmaid
I have seen it rendered slave woman
behold the slave woman of the lord

not sarah but hagar speaking to the angel
foreshadowing some dreadful apocalypse
a woman with child driven into wilderness

too much for an old half awake sleeper
better alleluias strung together like beads
raising the mind into stillness

our morning painted a solid blue
after a yesterday of darkening clouds

lines for a hand crafted book
poem for wendy allen

I will use them these pages
yes with care
I will not treat these
as if they could be bought

these are beyond commerce
kind hands smoothed these pages

these crafted gifts
so much skill in their making

how splendid to have them
and my years eight by ten
yes more than that now

I am happy wendy
given your own birthday
that I can thank you

with these lines
for my birthday pages

scratch out anything

what is it what is it
a loss of purpose
or talent gone to pieces
or just not having
anything to say
or the pain in the spine
or the fatigue
or the news on the radio
or some self loathing
beyond satisfaction

what is it what is it
well you started this thing
where are you going with it
down the page
the usual where
where else is there

the old days now
why you could brandish a torch
inscribe something wonderful
on some inner chamber
you found in a cave
with bisons or leopards

more interesting than
these decending lines

it is the fatigue
says you will never write again
and anyway who cares
who wants to read
your latest announcement
I don't know
perhaps someone like myself
sitting in a coffee shop
paging an anthology
selections yes from a book
filled with people you knew once

all gone now their efforts
keepsakes in these pages
come to mind again
karl shapiro telling me
u of chicago was a hell of an imprint
his wife shaking her head
someone wanting to know
did her husband speak in rhymes

what happened to this computer

so sensitive doesn't like the way I write
wants to cap the beginning of lines
has something of a victorian sensibility
now has underscored victorian
red lined the first victorian
insists on capping victorian
and what was victorian
why england when queen victoria
ruled from buckingham palace
now had red lined buckingham
has some thing about proper names
now wants to couple some thing
blue line under some thing
I know how I want to set out my lines
better than this obstinate mechanical brain
it gives you pause does it not
aha paws which do you choose computer
a temporary break in forward thrust
or a dog eared spate of lines

it used to be fanciful

what was it
the mind plays tricks
one distraction
the thread of thought breaks
and there you are
holding the loose ends
what were you thinking
what moment
danced in your imagination
I am just scratching lines here
trying to say something
that is worth remembering

speaking of being tired

why am I so tired
the doctor said it is old age
go home and get some sleep

I should be sleeping now
instead I am writing about it
poets are like this
the world falls out of orbit
and they all start epics
want to tell everybody about
what everybody already knows
they could at least
try with couplets

well this is about
all I can say about this
have a nice day

sometimes with little to say

what is there to say
when your confidence is exhausted
well there is a haunting song
"send in the clowns" that song
so attractive to so many singers
but then there are no clowns
who can repair so bleak a moment
yes restore a loss of faith
they can only distract for a moment
then they go tumbling off tumbling off
cartwheeling at some other circus
no you are left with yourself
what then

mail poem

friends let us all answer our mail
but tell the truth I have no complaint
I never had anything to say
all those old years at my desk
trying to think of something to say

you would suppose a writer
would be good at messages
but I never learned the art
making something so priceless

also people do not want to consider
your sublime pronouncements
they want to know how your dog is
and they prefer to tell you about their weather
and all the starlings in their yards

they do not care about your prizes either
if yours are better than theirs they smile grimly
if theirs are better than yours they smile grimly

there are exceptions of course
but I can't think of any at the moment
so I guess I should wind this thing up
maybe write a note to someone
or get started on a novel

if you are caught reading this
say you don't know me

sometimes you just keep writing

great cloud of ideas
blows over without rain
well enjoy the sunshine
the world is full of false starts
not to mention the people who make them
some are happy some not
some are bald some have hairy legs
well enough of this

it is the empty white space
you want to inhabit
make something out of nothing
it drives you up the wall
well the wall in the white space
you understand I imagine

it is a hollow in the belly
unholy waiting for baptism
crying the waters too cold
well this is how writers are
they don't get along with themselves
can't wait to tell everyone about it

so here is this page of stuff
have you read this far
if you have I have to say
not bad it could have been worse
and if you have not
well you can't say anything can you

words at the edge of time

blue asters suddenly
braving their october
and winter coming on

this morning what was done
a walk in the mall
a flu shot in the right arm

there was a purchase too
what prompted this
something sentimental perhaps

well I do not remember
I remember a strawberry scone
this at the bakery

a woman there
walking out of the past
with a hello and a smile

and my small house
it has been dusted and scoured
the carpets cleaned

what has been important here
not the small facts
but the words that gathered them

strawberry purchase mall
morning scone remember
carpet bakery winter scoured

the woman her greeting
the warm recognition in her smile

so many words here so priceless
handed down the generations
gathered on this page

appearing at the edge of time
holding against all that will come
this one moment
for whoever will see them

John Knoepfle

John Knoepfle was born in 1923 in Cincinnati, Ohio and has spent the last sixty years or so exploring in poetry and sometimes prose the places and times he has lived in. Among his many books, *Prayer Against Famine and Other Irish Poems,* published in 2003 by BkMk Press, places his search for his Irish ancestors in the context of contemporary struggles for justice and peace all over the world, including in Ireland. These themes and more personal ones of family and friendship shape his most recent books: *Walking in Snow,* a book of poetry, *I Look Around For My Life,* an autobiography, both published in 2008 by Pearn and Associates, as was *Shadows and Starlight,* also a book of poetry, in 2012.

    Knoepfle lives in Springfield, Illinois, with his wife, Peggy. He is an emeritus professor of literature at the University of Illinois Springfield. He says, "I try to scratch out a page of lines every morning." Of his computer, he says: "I despise the mouse."

Books by Pearn and Associates

Kindle
Cowboy Up: Kenny Sailors, The Jump Shot and Wyoming's Championship Basketball History, Ryan Thorburn
Lost Cowboys: The Story of Bud Daniel and Wyoming Baseball, Ryan Thorburn
Black 14: The Rise, Fall and Rebirth of Wyoming Football, Ryan Thorburn
Ikaria: A Love Odyssey on a Greek Island and *Ever After,* Anita Sullivan
I Look Around for my Life, John Knoepfle
The Great Adventure—Untold, Charles Hamman
The Bridge of Isfahan, Nilla Cram Cook
Halfway to Eternity, Michael Scott Stevens
1945, Joseph J. Kozma
It Started & Ended, Bud Grounds
Love is like a Lizard, Dr. Jerry Gibson

Nonfiction
Love is like a Lizard, Dr. Jerry Gibson
A Lenten Journey Toward Christian Maturity, William E. Breslin
 (also available in Spanish: *Tiempo de Cuaresma a Traves de Madurez Cristiana*)
Black 14, Lost Cowboys, and *Cowboy Up,* Ryan Thorburn
Goulash and Picking Pickles, Louise Mae Hoffmann
Ikaria: A Love Odyssey on a Greek Island, Anita Sullivan
I Look Around for my Life, John Knoepfle
It Started & Ended: The Story About a Soldier and Civilian Life, Bud Grounds
The Great Adventure—Untold, Charles Hamman

Fiction
The Bridge of Isfahan, Nilla Cram Cook
Halfway to Eternity, Michael Scott Stevens
1945, Joseph J. Kozma
Ever After, Anita Sullivan

Poetry
Then She Kissed El Paco's Lips Now! Or April in DeKalb, Ricardo Mario Amezquita
Mathematics in Color, Until We Meet, and *The New Neanderthal,* Joseph J Kozma
The Dreamer and the Dream, Rick E. Roberts
Walking in Snow, and *Shadows and Starlight,* John Knoepfle

www.ingramcontent.com/pod-product-compliance
Lightning Source LLC
Chambersburg PA
CBHW031243160426
43195CB00009BA/579